Expressive Etudes

TRADITIONAL STUDIES FOR ARTISTIC DEVELOPMENT AT THE PIANO

Book Two

Late Elementary

Compiled and edited by
Suzanne W. Guy

Practice Suggestions

Posture is critical to good technique. Sit tall and centered on the front part of the bench.

- **Prepare yourself physically using this checklist:**

shoulders   Roll your shoulders forward and back several times. Now lift them toward your ears and let them fall comfortably into place.

upper arms   Dangle your arms at your sides while seated at the piano. Lift them slowly in front of you, parallel to the floor, then drop them freely in your lap.

forearms   Move your forearms rapidly from side to side (similar to erasing), then up and down (as if hammering a nail). You are using horizontal and vertical motion.

wrists   Hold your R.H. fingertips snugly in the palm of your L.H. and move the wrist down and up (repeat several times and then reverse hands). Use this gesture to begin and end phrases.

fingers   Imagine pressing a thumb tack into a cork board with a firm fingertip. First joints should be strong and not collapse.

- **Scan the etude to find the specific technical elements used by the composer.** Practice them slowly and accurately.

- **Notice and observe all markings on the page:** character and tempo indications, dynamics, articulation, and phrase lengths. Attention to these details will bring the etude to life and make it more expressive.

- **Determine a reasonable practice tempo from the most difficult measures.** Then play through the entire etude until it flows.

- **Practice your etude at three different tempi:** slow–medium–fast. A good rule to follow is "two times slow for one time fast."

- **Work at your own tempo and pace,** always playing music, not just the notes. Remember to stress the beauty of the sound, which is more important than speed. Your technical fluency will increase as you continue to practice.

- **Use your imagination.** A scale might represent a beautiful melody sung by your favorite singer. A chord could portray the approach of a powerful dragon. An arpeggio might be a fountain. Come up with your own ideas.

Enjoy the challenges and rewards of etude practice.

Expressive Etudes
Book Two – *Late Elementary*

Table of Contents

FF1298

Bagatelle

R.H. extended hand position; L.H. repeated chord accompaniment

Anton Diabelli
(1781–1858)

Etude, Op. 101, No. 60

(Preparatory School)

Imitation; parallel and contrary motion

Ferdinand Beyer
(1803–1863)

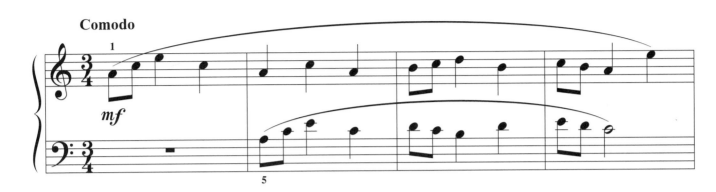

The Chase, Op. 117, No. 15

(The First Lessons)

Two-note slurs; R.H. rotation

Cornelius Gurlitt
(1820–1901)

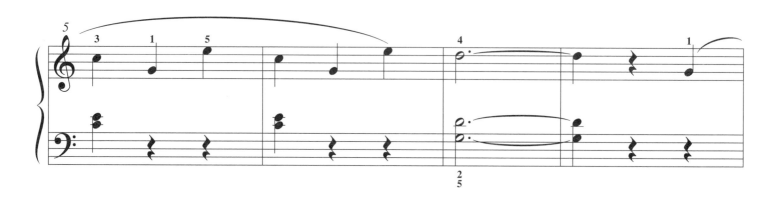

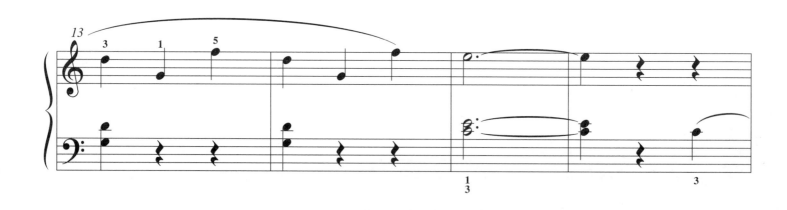

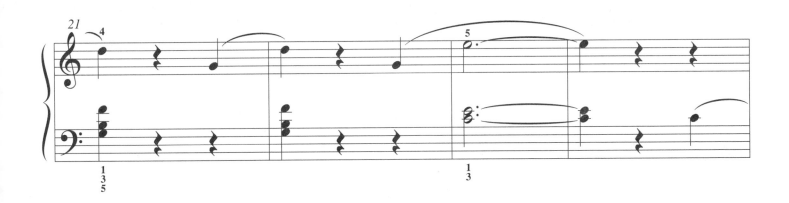

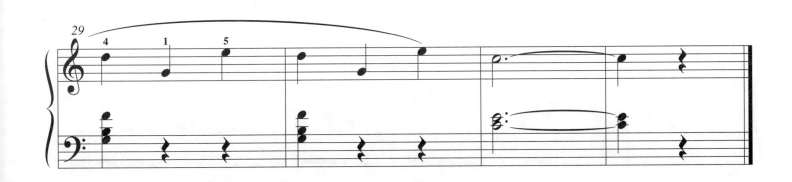

8

Study, Op. 176, No. 3

(25 Elementary Studies)

Cantabile melody; broken-chord accompaniment

Jean-Baptiste Duvernoy
(1802–1880)

FF1298

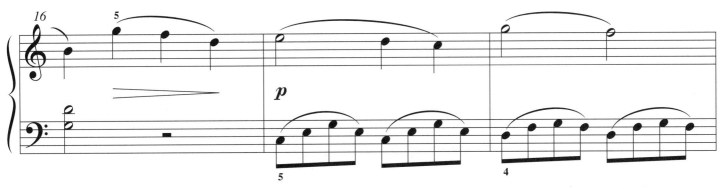

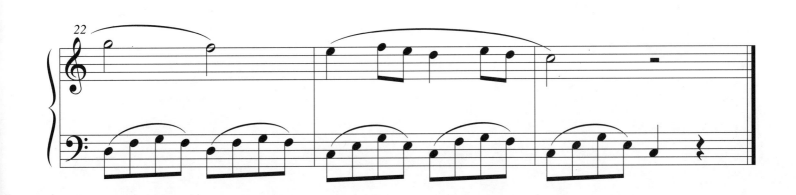

Etude, Op. 599, No. 19

(Practical Method for Beginners)

R.H. scale passagework; primary chord accompaniment; balance

Carl Czerny
(1791–1857)

Etude, Op. 777, No. 8

(Five-finger Studies)

Contrasting articulation; broken-chord accompaniment

Carl Czerny
(1791–1857)

Etude, Op. 777, No. 22

(Five-finger Studies)

Grace notes; contrasting articulation; waltz accompaniment

Carl Czerny
(1791–1857)

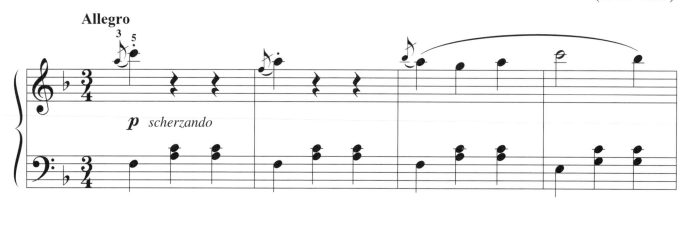

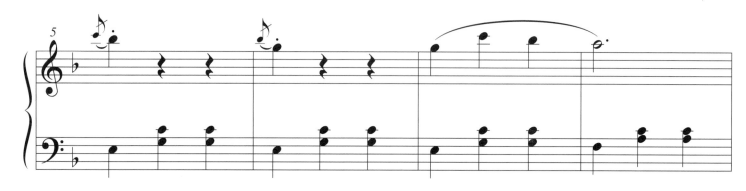

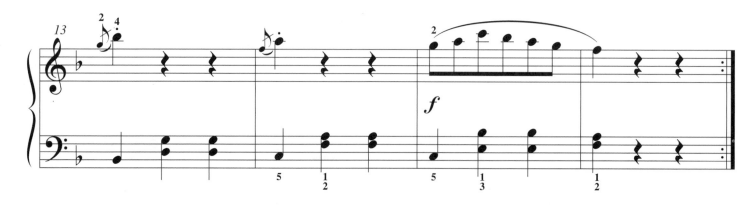

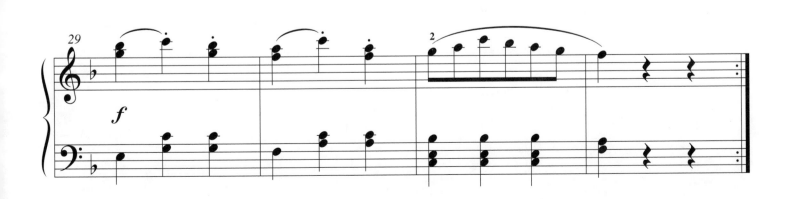

Etude, Op. 82, No. 39

(The First Steps of the Young Pianist)

L.H. cantabile melody; L.H. octaves

Cornelius Gurlitt
(1820–1901)

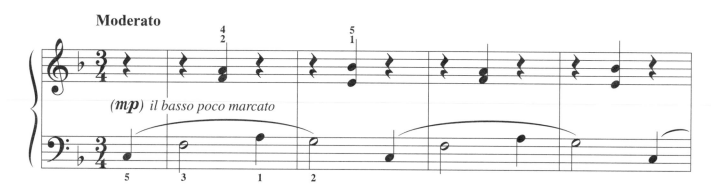

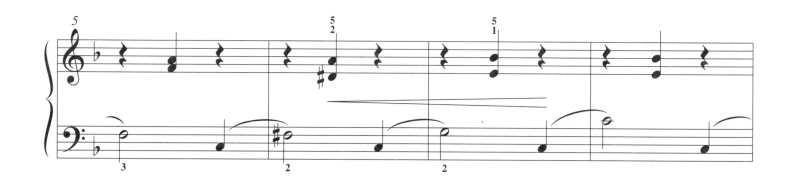

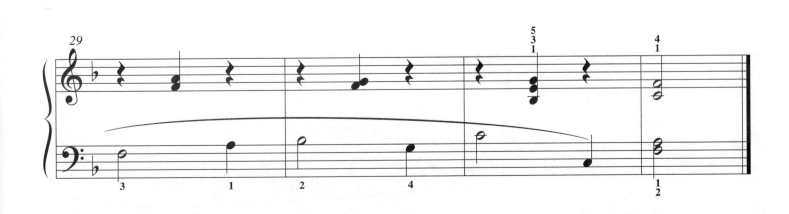

Etude, Op. 82, No. 65

(The First Steps of the Young Pianist)

Extended hand position with crossovers; legato melody; quick, repeated intervals

Cornelius Gurlitt
(1820–1901)

Village Dance

(From one of Beethoven's sketchbooks)

Three–voice part writing; bass pedal point transposition

Ludwig van Beethoven
(1770–1827)

Etude, Op. 108, No. 12

(25 Melodious Studies)

Melody in bass; repeated chord accompaniment

Ludvig Schytte
(1848–1909)

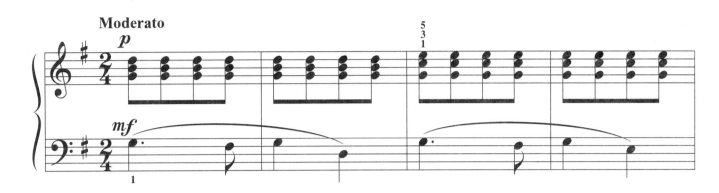

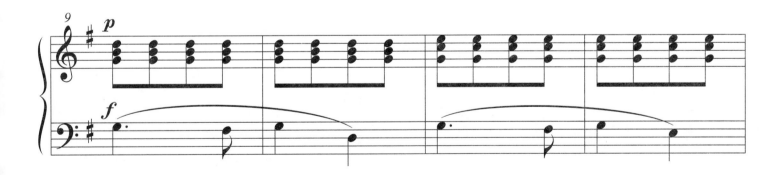

Etude, Op. 108, No. 5

(25 Melodious Studies)

Two-note slurs in perpetual motion; harmonic pedaling

Ludvig Schytte
(1848–1909)

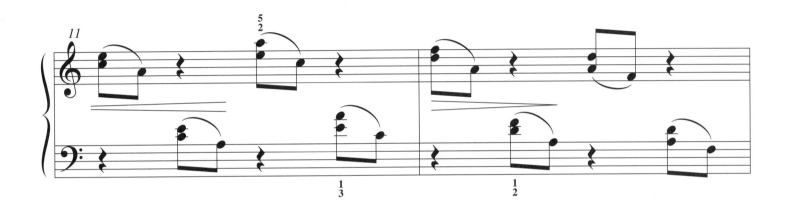

Impatience, Op. 13, No. 6

(12 Little Fantasy Studies)

Repeated notes; changing fingers

Alec Rowley
(1892–1958)

Etude, Op. 218, No. 34

(Children's Exercises and Melodies)

Ascending and descending scales; contrasting articulations

Louis Köhler
(1820–1886)

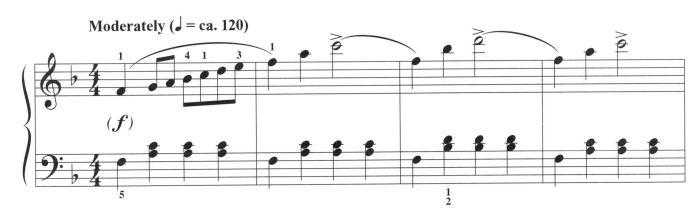

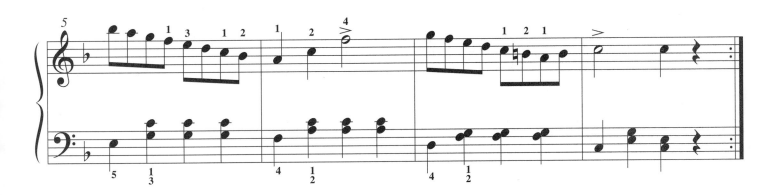

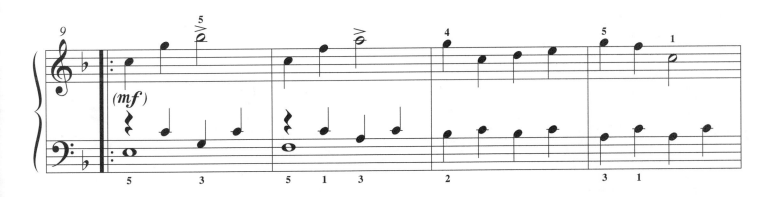

A Pleasant Morning, Op. 63, No. 1

(12 Melodious Pieces, Book 1)

Scale passagework; cantabile melody; L.H. emphasis (mm 25–29)

Jean Louis Streabbog
(1835–1886)

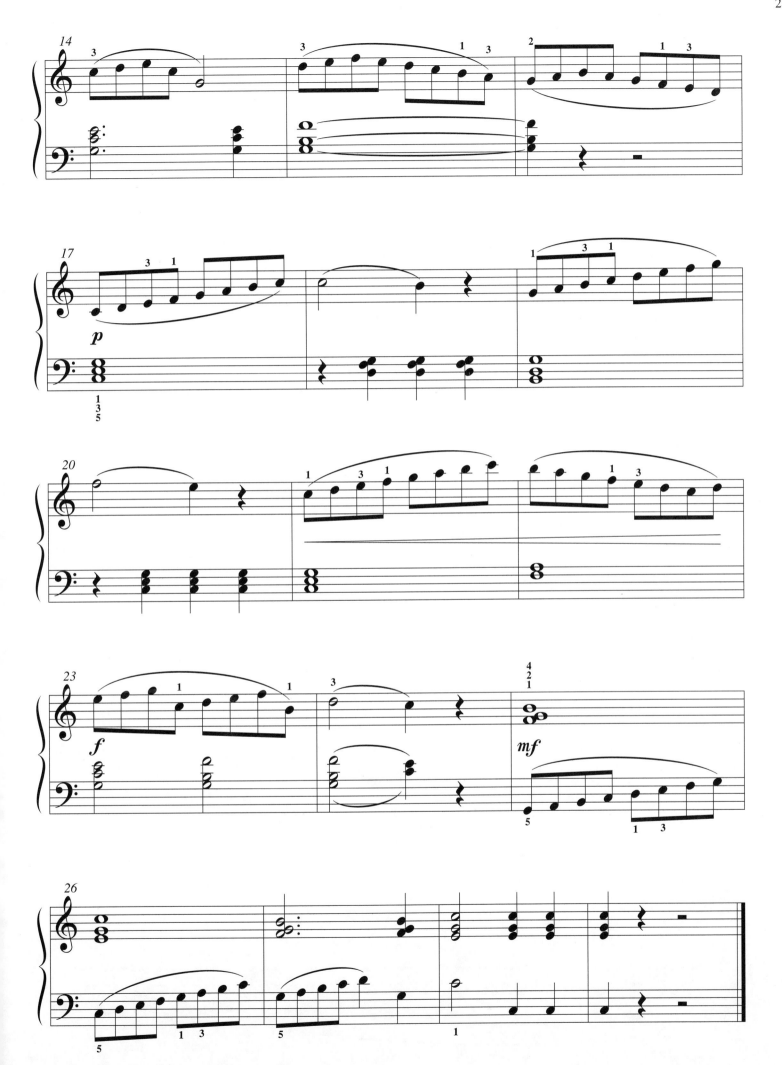

Little Piece, Op. 68, No. 5

(Album for the Young)

Cantabile melody; balance and rotation; L.H. melody hidden in accompaniment

Robert Schumann
(1810–1856)

Nicht schnell (not fast)

Etude, Op. 17, No. 18

(The Alphabet—25 Very Easy Studies)

R.H. and L.H. crossovers; harmonic pedaling

Felix Le Couppey
(1811–1887)

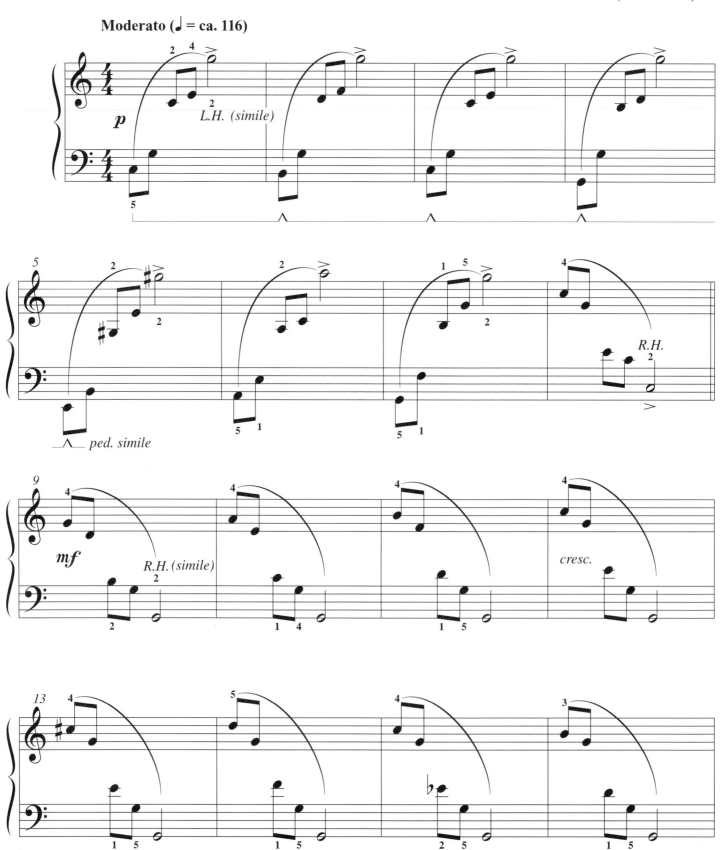

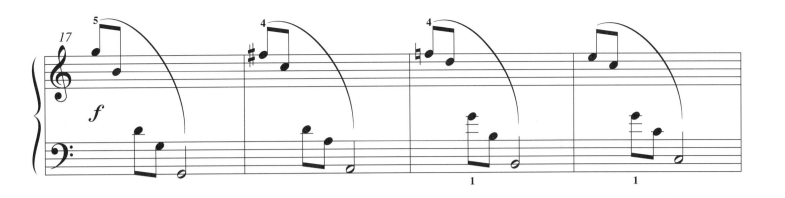

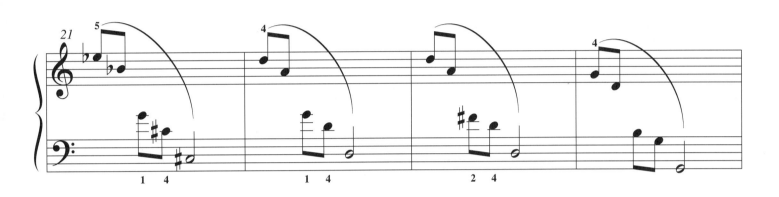

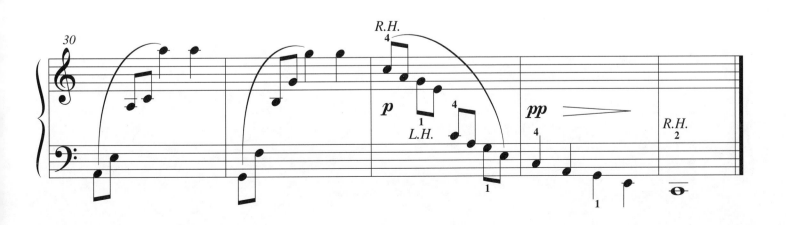

Minuet

(First Term at the Piano)

Double sixths; loose, relaxed wrists; contrasting articulation

Béla Bartók
(1881–1945)

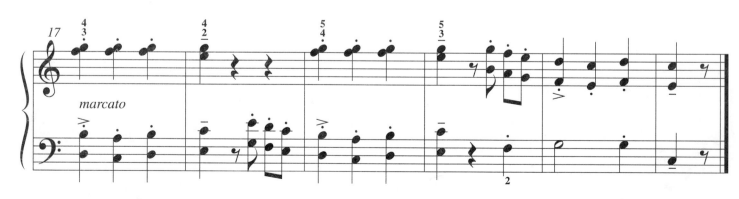

Composer Biographies

Béla Bartók (1881–1945, Hungary) One of the most original composers of the early 20th century, Bartók was also a pianist, teacher, linguist, ethnomusicologist, and editor. He wrote music from the elementary to the virtuosic level, including three piano concerti. His pedagogical masterpiece *Mikrokosmos* is a laboratory of 153 miniature pieces incorporating his technical ideas and ethnic spirit.

Ludwig van Beethoven (1770–1827, Germany) Trained in both piano and violin, and recognized as an outstanding pianist and teacher, Beethoven's first composition (a set of variations) was published at age 12. Through the extraordinary range of his nine symphonies, 32 piano sonatas, and landmark chamber music compositions, Beethoven's universal appeal is recognized daily—whether it's through a *Peanuts* cartoon, at a concert featuring a Beethoven composition, or a student practicing a favorite piece.

Ferdinand Beyer (1803–1863, Germany) In addition to writing a popular beginning method (used in Korea until 1970), Beyer was also known for his deft arrangements of opera themes and transcriptions of orchestral works. Little known today, Beyer was a respected Romantic composer during his lifetime.

Carl Czerny (1791–1857, Austria) This piano teacher, pianist, and writer composed over a thousand compositions and holds the distinction of writing more exercises and etudes than any other composer. As a pupil of Beethoven and the primary teacher of Liszt, Czerny occupies a unique historical place in the development of piano technique. His technical pieces ensure his legacy.

Anton Diabelli (1781–1858, Austria) Known as the publisher of both Schubert and Beethoven's music, Diabelli composed 11 keyboard sonatinas and many melodic pieces for the young. He was especially concerned with music education and spearheaded a contest for composers to submit variations on his original waltz theme.

Jean-Baptiste Duvernoy (1802–1880, France) Although a lesser–known French composer, pianist, and teacher, Duvernoy was interested in the development of piano technique from the earliest levels up to and including intermediate–level piano studies in Op. 120. The 25 etudes in Op. 176 are especially appealing to young pianists.

Cornelius Gurlitt (1820–1901, Austria) An outstanding organist and composer, Gurlitt composed chamber music that included song cycles, a cello sonata, and three violin sonatas. The lyricism in Gurlitt's technical compositions, suggestive of Robert Schumann, appeals to students of all ages.

Louis Köhler (1820–1886, Germany) This German pianist, composer, and pedagogue established a successful piano school. His keyboard studies, considered on a par with Czerny, were favorites of students in European music schools due to their simplicity and directness. He was especially fond of scales and repeated patterns.

Felix Le Couppey (1811–1887, France) A man of many talents, Le Couppey was a pianist, teacher, composer, and publisher. He wrote several piano methods while teaching piano and harmony at the Paris Conservatory. His etudes, character pieces, and songs are lyrical as well as technical.

Alec Rowley (1892–1958, England) Composer, pianist, and English teacher, Rowley was committed to the musical education of young people. He was half of a concertizing duet team and wrote several concerti for solo instruments and orchestra. His fantasy studies have a distinctive style and sound.

Robert Schumann (1810–1856, Germany) In addition to composing symphonies, a concerto, chamber music, and a large body of piano tone poems, Schumann founded a literary journal that railed against the "lightweight" salon music of his day. Even his simplest compositions (from *Album for the Young*) bear the mark of a complex composer—counterpoint, dotted rhythms, and unusual harmonies.

Ludvig Schytte (1848–1909, Denmark) Although he began his career as a pharmacist, Schytte's musical talent developed rapidly from the age of 22. A skilled pianist, he studied with Franz Liszt and taught at several conservatories in Vienna. He became interested in composition, mastering miniature forms and publishing more than 200 pieces. The etudes from Op. 108 and 160 are the most familiar.

Jean Louis Streabbog (1835–1886, Belgium) This prolific composer and pianist who taught at the Brussels Conservatory wrote more than a thousand light piano pieces. Streabbog is the pen name for Gobbaerts (spelling it in reverse). Nearly all piano students cut their technical teeth on the melodious studies in Op. 63. Because they were so popular, he wrote a second set in Op. 64 (which was less successful).